MW00412083

ZERO TO A MILLION
(WITHOUT SHOWING YOUR BUTTHOLE)

BY

SARAH AND JOSH BOWMAR

ZERO TO A MILLION

Ordering Information: Quantity sales. Special discounts are available on quantity purchases by corporations, associations, and others. Orders by U.S. trade bookstores and wholesalers. Please contact Sarah and Josh Bowmar.

DREAMSTARTERS

Edited and Marketed By DreamStarters University
www.DreamStartersUniversity.com

Table of Contents

Behind the Title

Why, "Zero to a Million Without Showing Your Butthole?"

While some might do a double-take or chuckle when they hear the title of this book, it's very deliberate, and I hope an ultimately empowering title, especially for women.

Too often, in today's world, women choose to use their bodies to market a blog, video channel, Instagram or other business tool. How many times have you seen this?

Maybe the title of this book will turn some people off, but for many of us, especially women, I think it will resonate. To get from zero to a million followers, you don't have to go that route. This book will show you how to gain a following by having meaningful content, conversations, and connections with your followers.

You don't have to wear a thong to gain a social media presence. It takes a lot more work, it's more methodical, it takes more thought to do it without using your sexuality- but it can be done. That's also not to demonize women who choose to go this route- this book is simply to empower those who do not want to take their clothes off. These principles can also be applied to men as well- it can be difficult for men to gain a following in the fitness world- but it certainly is not impossible.

4

To gain the following (and an influence), there are certain steps you need to take, and that's where this book will take you. It's certainly not easy work but it is simple- consistency will be your best friend.

A little history about my social media "start:" It surprises people sometimes when I tell them that my very first Instagram posts were of a cupcake and my cats (if you already follow me, this will not be of a surprise)! In fact, I resisted the whole Instagram thing as long as I could. For me, it was just one more thing to keep updated. I was working at a digital marketing agency when I started mine and keep in mind, this is in the ancient times of Instagram when there were no stories, no videos, no highlights, no swipes - it was just photos.

My first year on Instagram, I was a dairy and egg free vegetarian and competing in NPC bikini contests. It was so challenging hitting my protein to get the look and energy that I needed and I have always loved to cook. This forced me to be very creative in the kitchen and I started sharing my healthy and fun recipes on my page! Foods like low-carb pancakes, high protein donuts, etc really gained a lot of traction and interest and the followers started coming. Sharing recipes is something I still do and now I have two cookbooks that have over 200 pages each on top of everything else we do.

I initially focused on providing value for my followers, and still do. I am constantly seeking how I can do things better, how I can provide better content, how I can provide better products and services, and how I can support those who support me. I truly at the end of the day want to help as many people as possible. My mantra has always been to leave the world in a better place than I found it.

All I've learned about Instagram didn't come from a book or a class. It came from building things up, making a lot of mistakes, learning from those mistakes, as well as learning from what I was doing right. I was, and still am, a student of my craft. I am always open to trying new things, learning by reading another persons' work on this topic, or that field. I listen to podcasts while I'm driving on this subject; there's so much information out there, and so much to learn. Turn your care into a traveling university. I've built relationships with others who have a large following, and we bounce tips and ideas off each other. No matter your past or your upbringing, you can make your future whatever you want. To paraphrase Bill Gates, your past is not your fault, but your future is absolutely your responsibility.

Josh, when he was just getting started, traded his services with a prominent real-estate expert to learn about running a successful business, even though that professional was more than willing to pay Josh for his personal training work. Josh taught him a lot on the fitness side, and that real-estate and businessman, Michael Drew, taught Josh a lot about the business side. Josh also attended a lot of formal business training workshops and sessions, read every book that he could find since he felt he had a lot to learn, coming from a background where there wasn't a lot of business knowledge, and he realized that the best way he could help his struggling family, after the 2008 economic downturn, was to become a business owner, and do it right.

I hope that, with this book, I can help you improve your life by being true to yourself and helping others. If you follow the steps outlined and do the work, I bet you will. I would love to hear from you in a year from now, telling me how much your life has changed and all about how you're changing lives.

I don't ever look at our followers and fans as dollar bills. I don't look at any follower and say, "Ok, that person is worth x, y or z to me." They would feel that. I genuinely want to help people. That should also be a goal for you: genuinely wanting to help and make a difference. Communicating my passion is the best way to build a following that will pay you back in ways you can only begin to dream.

Let's get started.

"If you want people to be interested, you have to be interesting."

SARAH & JOSH BOWMAR

Chapter 1

How to Have an Influence, Not Just a Following

I see this all the time in the fitness world, but in other fields as well. Someone with an active Instagram account has a lot of followers but doesn't really offer much of anything for their followers to grab ahold of. There aren't a lot of video, content, or links to keep a connection going with the follower. In short, their Instagram, though maybe flashy at first, doesn't help anyone in the long run.

Let's take the fitness industry, for example. Someone's page might just have posts that are photos of their body; there are no recipes, no workout tips, no information that someone can actually use. Instead of engaging with the follower, who might be asking, "Hey, you look great, and you feel great...how can you help me look and feel great, too?"

This might sound silly, but we take it very seriously. Whatever we create in our business, including the content on the website, or the Instagram page, we want it to help people in some way. Having this type of focus helps us stay interesting and relevant. If we ask ourselves, every time we add content, "How is this going to help someone," it helps us influence someone who is wanting to make a positive change in their lives.

You'll see it in the comments. Instead of freaky, sexual comments, we see a dialogue going. You see our followers sharing ideas with us and with each other. You go beyond the entertainment value of the post and start digging into the real value of any post. At the end of the day, you might sometimes ask yourself who has had an influence over you, and it's usually someone who has helped you. And this is the key. Be the person that helps someone else, even if it's someone who you have never met, and may possibly never meet. You can reach each and every one of your followers if you take the time to post things that are influential and meaningful.

But, here's the real key.....to have an influence on those who are following you on Instagram, for example, you have to create an environment where your followers feel like you are helping more than you're taking from them. If they get the sense that you're just using them to get money from them, they will abandon you in a second. Instagram followers are savvy, in general. They can sniff a potential cheat a mile away. They have great BS detectors. If you're not offering true value, and you're just using the follower base to think of you like a sleazy used car salesman, and - poof - there goes your influence.

The Law of Reciprocation really comes into play here. You may or may not be familiar with this law, so now's a good chance to review or introduce it, because it's at the heart of this entire book, and especially this particular lesson.

Whenever you are ever talking about having an influence, and making money from that influence, how that works is through the Law of Reciprocation. Once you get an influence, which is gained by helping people (without asking for anything in return) those same people will feel like they have to give back to you - in some way, shape or form. You've made a difference in their life, they are going to ask themselves how they can help you. So, that's when they buy your supplements, your services, your ebook, your program, whatever your product is.

The most common mistake I think people make is that they lead with the sale. "Buy my stuff, buy my stuff, buy my stuff," without actually helping their audience. The ratio of helping and influencing to selling and buying is extremely sensitive. In some ways, you have to give so much away for free, to gain that influence. This all takes time and effort.

For example, I publish recipes, tips to get fit, exercise videos, full workouts, transformations, motivational tips, full meal ideas, podcast links, articles, helpful videos, etc. I interact by responding to DMs and comments - this easily takes up 3-4 hours each day, but building these relationships and trust with my followers is critical.

It happens all the time when we meet people at expos or conferences. They'll say to me, "You are the only one who responded to me, and I can't even believe it because you have such a large following. It's so cool that you actually take the time, and you care." That's something that's so important to me. I'll DM athletes that I want to sponsor, and they won't even respond. Really. Do you think you're that above others that you can't even respond? I want my followers to feel like I do care and that I can help them in some way, and that no matter how "big" I get, I will take the time to respond and help.

Let me tell you something now, too. Once you get that large number of followers, you can't stop caring. Don't get duped into thinking you're more important than you really are. No matter how large that number is, you never have the right to be rude and to be a jerk. You have an obligation, I think, to stay connected, to keep the conversation going. You'll find that in the short term it's very satisfying, and in the long-term, it will only help your business and monetary goals. Ask yourself this question....would you really want to give your money to someone you think is a jerk? Or, are you more likely to give your hard-earned money to someone you know genuinely cares about you?

You have to go above and beyond. You have to stay humble and think of yourself as a normal person (because you are). You have to stay sincere. Don't be afraid to share what you know! That's how you can help people the most. If you're just being lazy, and posting a picture of yourself in your underwear, or a bible verse, or a lame quote like, "work hard," that's easy. And lazy. It's NOT easy creating meaningful content that helps people, commenting back when people ask questions, responding to DMs and doing that every day - no matter what. All for nothing in return. You're not selling your recipes, or your content, or your workout tips. That level of work turns a lot of people off. They want the shortcut to likes and high follower numbers. Likes don't pay the bills. Likes don't allow you to self-fund your business.

So, how did I find myself here? What was a turning point in my life and experience that led me to build an influencing presence on Instagram? How did I come to define myself as an influencer?

When I met my husband, Josh, I was on a completely different path. Yes, I was doing fitness, I already had 100,000 followers on Instagram, but I was working in the corporate world. I have my undergrad and Masters in marketing and luckily found a job in my field at a digital marketing agency in Toledo, OH. I was doing fitness as a hobby, just something to give me some extra spending cash. I never thought it would be my full-time job. I never saw myself as a business owner.

Fast forward to the Arnold Sports Festival in 2014 in Columbus. I was getting ready for a show and needed to lift after the expo. There weren't many 24 hour gyms near downtown but I ended up finding one. It was a Saturday night and my intent was to just lift- I had my hat on, headphones in, "don't talk to me" written all over my face.

Unknown to me, Josh was watching me the whole time, in my polka-dotted work out pants, and plotting a "water fountain meet up." Apparently, every time I would walk toward the water fountain, Josh would get ready to make his move, but I would make a quick turn to one of the workout machines, foiling his plans. Finally, he just came up to me, while I was working out - a huge gym etiquette no-no - and introduced himself.

I bring this up because one of our first conversations at the gym was about the usual "what do you do." I told him about my corporate career ladder, education, etc., and turned to him, "What do you do?" He told me, "Well, I do the fitness thing full-time." I didn't even think that was possible! Both my parents are very traditional when it comes to career, so I did not have that entrepreneurial mindset, even though I had pursued certifications as a personal trainer and was fitness nutrition certified. This was all as a hobby since people had reached out to me to help them with their own fitness goals. But, when I met Josh, he really pushed me to pursue my passion full-time.

Josh had already been developing things like workout plans, online programs, on a smaller scale than we are doing now, of course. He wanted time and money, and for that, he says, "you have to have systems." So, he was doing group training, working with up to 10 people at a time, maximizing money for his time. He had also developed two-day systems to help families build workout routines, develop meal plans, go shopping, etc. All of this was still taking too much time and effort, because it was such a small, niche market. It was hard to build it into something bigger.

While he was doing that, he was also selling online programs to people with his Instagram following of 10-15,000. He didn't have the marketing skills that I had learned, so he was a great salesman, worked hard, and had the systems in place. I had the marketing skills, but not the systems, so when we combined efforts, we learned how to make our Instagram accounts meaningful, interesting, valuable to our followers, and resulting in a lucrative business.

You wouldn't believe how many people let us know that once they got fit, they got a raise or a new relationship, or their marriage got better, or they gained more confidence. In fact, not too long ago, we got a care package from two former

15

ZERO TO A MILLION

clients (Curtis and Kianna Miller) who, after attending one of our couples challenges, meeting us at the Arnold convention, and working the systems that we teach, shared how they opened their own gym, and now have 800 members. Sometimes it amazes how the simple work we do, like posting workouts, recipes, sharing business strategies, can have a snowball effect on people's lives. That's what being an influencer is all about.

Have something to offer, and a story especially if you can show a transformation. The story doesn't need to be a struggle to triumph, necessarily, but just something you overcame. That can really help motivate someone because everyone is struggling in some way. So, if you can show how you overcame something, that can be absolutely huge. And, be relatable. You have to be able to bridge the gap from where someone is to where they want to be. You have to know the steps on how to get there.

Influencers are leaders, and a good leader is confident. The only way to gain confidence is to be humble, learn from your mistakes, be willing to keep working at it and become more and more confident. No one practicing a new skill wakes up a master. No one looking to get fit wakes up "shredded." No, it takes time and confidence. Being an influencer is allowing that confidence to shine. Confidence is not a talent, it's a skill. So that confidence has to practiced and honed.

You'll be confident in anything with repetition, repetition, repetition.

Right now, in my life, I hope to be an influencer so that people know we want to make the world a better place. Through the content that we post, the supplements we create, we strive to make a positive difference in peoples' lives. I want someone to think of us and say, "those people helped me." I want to help people become the best version of themselves that they can be. Because, let's face it, most people when they look in the mirror, it doesn't correlate with how they feel about themselves. How you actually feel and look are usually two different things. When you can marry those two things, where someone likes how they look AND feel, that can positively affect all areas of their lives.

Homework

Everybody is consistent at something. Even if it's a harmful or wasteful habit, we're still consistent at doing these things on a daily basis. Take five minutes to write down a list of things that you have committed to being consistent to. Once written down, take a look at what serves you and what doesn't. What are you doing on a daily basis that is working for you, and what are you doing on a daily basis that is working against you?

_____

_____

_____

_____

_____

_____

_____

_____

_____

_____

_____

_____

_____

"80-85% of your core content needs to be what you're interested in, what you're an expert about, and what you're passionate about."

Chapter 2

Have a Specific Interest or Hobby and Stick to it

If you're looking to change lives, and find a way to monetize that through Instagram, this point is critical. You don't necessarily make money from what you're passionate about, but you can make money, and help people, by sharing what you know about your passions. For example, I love to fish. Will I make a million dollars cooking? Probably not. But, I can make money talking about cooking, teaching techniques, and tips, and sharing information on cooking healthy recipes.

Here the focus is really important. If you have a following about gardening, for example, don't push a lot of posts about fitness. Remember who your audience is and why

20

they're following you in the first place. If you have multiple interests that you want to post on, think about separating those. A very real example, if we post something about being outdoors and hunting, but on our fitness page, we can immediately lose 5,000 - 10,000 followers. Try to get those followers back. You can't. They're gone, probably forever.

For our outdoor and hunting activities, we have a separate channel and a separate Instagram account. We understand that bow hunting can be a sensitive topic which is why we have separated the two. However, we do our best to educate our followers on the importance of conservation. We also always bring hunting back to result in a fitness related discussion by consuming the meat that we hunt that ultimately fuels our body.

The bottom line is that if you're good at two different things, and you want to try and monetize that, you should create two separate social platforms. We are known by a lot of people for our work on the fitness front. We are also known for our posts related to hunting and specifically bow hunting, with top rated YouTube channels and Instagram accounts. I have to make sure that when I create content, that I'm not trying to marry these two very different worlds, because I will lose followers, and confuse people. Hunting is hunting. Fitness is fitness. And, even though they intersect in my own life, I can't, and shouldn't assume, they will intersect in someone else's life.

You never want your followers to feel bad- that should always be a goal. We might post twice a year on our fitness page, pictures or content about the meat that we harvest, using a bow and arrow. But, I wouldn't show, for example, the animal laying there. On the fitness page, I might show the tenderloins, and comment on how we are harvesting and eating organic meat. Now, on the hunting page, I do post information and pictures on the process, the hunting, the hard work that's involved in harvesting meat from the wild. Two different audiences. Two different approaches and very different content.

Same thing on the hunting page. If I were to post more than twice a year something related to fitness, I would alienate followers, and make someone feel bad. That's definitely not the goal. If we have followers who are out of shape, but who are on our hunting page, they are not seeking out fitness information by being on our hunting page. If we harp on the importance of fitness on the wrong page, we are pointing out something that someone may be very sensitive about, and it will make them feel bad. If someone is seeking out information on fitness, it's ok if we point things out related to fitness. They are looking for specific information in that realm.

If you want your Instagram to pay you, you do have to treat it like a full-time job. A lot of people don't do that. They don't take the time to respond to comments or DMs. As stated earlier- responding to as many people as you can to make those connections is a part of your "full time Instagram job".

You absolutely have to be passionate about the topic you're talking about. If you're not, your followers will see right through that. That passionate also makes it feel less like work. But, you can't confuse having fun, or the lack of, with what's important to maintain on your page. It's not fun responding to DMs, or posting replies, or writing out the same answers to the same questions. But, it's work, and it's important. If you're passionate about helping, people will feel and sense that. Those will be your most dedicated followers. They are following you because THEY are passionate about the subject, so you better be, too.

Be prepared to answer repetitive comments and questions and assume that each person has good intentions. It may sometimes not feel like it, but their passion for the content is what might be pushing them to be negative, or even rude. Sometimes that "rude" person is someone who is truly very new about the topic, or maybe English isn't their first language. Maybe them being "rude" is really because they don't know how to communicate. Always remember that everyone can see how you respond and react. People will judge you based on how you respond and this can either hurt you or help you- so be cautious.

I'm not perfect at this. I am not. This is something that I continually work on and am aware of as I share my passions with the world. It's most important to remember that it takes a long time to get a raving fan and just one negative comment to lose that same fan. Those fans are unbelievably valuable, so that's why it's so important to not lose them. It's the same reason you would keep two different industries or hobbies separate. A raving fan isn't going to put up with, or even be interested, in any passion that is different than why they joined your page in the first place.

One way to make sure you are finding your audience, especially as you are getting started, is to use strategic hashtags. Once you get established, you don't have to do this as much. But, in the beginning, I hashtagged almost every post. If you look on my page now, you'll rarely see a hashtag, because the audience has already been established. But, when people are first pursuing information about their passion, the hashtags can lead them to you, and to what you are offering. It can clutter things, so you don't have to put your hashtag in the caption, but you can still put it in the first comment on each post.

You can't just slap a hashtag on a post that's not really relevant, though. You have to have the content first, and then the hashtags can and will help you get more followers. Again, this goes back to the topic, and to the passion that you're trying to communicate. If your post doesn't match that passion that you're trying to tap into, you're just wasting time, and you'll turn off potential followers. Your top nine posts have to be relevant. Everyone who is going to check out your Instagram feed is going to scroll, with their thumb, and see your 9 most recent posts. If those posts don't have the content that they're looking for, they'll move on and never visit again.

That content has to be meaty. If I come across a fitness page, and 9 out of 10 posts are selfies, but not videos, or workout tips, or recipes or another meaningful and helpful content, I'm going to move on really quickly. Or, if someone I've followed all of a sudden starts muddling their feed with completely unrelated posts, or politics, or is just drifting away from the reason I followed them in the first place, I'm gone. And, I'm not going to, three months later, say to myself, "Gee, I wonder if so-and-so has improved the quality of their feed?" No. Gone and forgotten. We're all just one post away from being irrelevant or in big trouble. Not to scare you, but it's that important to give thought to each post.

This is where Instagram's ability to tell stories can come into play. That way you can tell a story through less significant posts, where it might not be worth its own post, but can be part of the story. If you're not familiar with Instagram stories, it's a great way to engage with your followers, and keep them involved with you for 24 hours. Stories are snippet posts that you string together, and the final "story" only stays on your page for 24 hours at a time. They don't stay on your Instagram feed after those 24 hours, either. So, it won't affect the "Top 9" posts that I talked about earlier. Once you have a fan base, there can be a lot of fun and excitement about the live and timely content that stories offer. Use them to your advantage, and have fun!

Homework

Take a look at your Instagram feed, and judge it on the following points. (Remember to do this as if you are not you, but someone seeing your page for the VERY FIRST TIME!)

Can someone tell the main focus of my page by just looking at those most recent 9-10 posts? If not, why not?

Does your summary draw people in? Would you follow you? Why or why not?

Visit your top-three Instagram pages that you visit, and that you're a raving fan of. What is it about those pages that keep you coming back? Ask yourself what it is you love about that page and what is it that keeps you coming back? What do you need to do on your page to bring that same passion front-and-center?

Do the above, and you'll come up with some great questions and answers about what YOU should be posting, or what you shouldn't be posting. Don't be afraid to mirror what someone else is doing that you like. You'll eventually find your own voice, and people will be copying you.

"You have to post and know WHY you're posting."

Chapter 3

Be a Professional Phoneographer

Most phones these days are actually cameras that happen to make phone calls, and this makes social media so fun and easy. It seems natural in today's world to take photos of everyday moments. Some people are nervous about whether or not the photo is of high enough quality but don't fret about that, either. There are great free apps that can help bring out the best in your photos without you having to spend a lot of time fine-tuning and improving the quality of your photographs.

One app that I use all the time is Snapseed. It's especially good with the sunset or other outdoor scenes, as it actually makes the photo look like what you saw in real life. Honestly, how many times have you taken a photo of the sunset or the moon, and when you look at it you shake your head, because it just didn't do it. The lighting is off or something looks blurry. Snapseed takes care of that, and it's really easy to use.

When it comes to content and posting photos, you can spend hours and hours on Photoshop to post the perfect picture. But, in the meantime, you only have time to post something every other day because you're spending so much time editing your pictures. Instead, use an app like Snapseed, and turn your quality photos into high-quality photos that are, literally, good enough. Remember, that the entire focus is to post high-quality content, and the photo just has to be good enough to support the content, so you can post often and keep your followers engaged.

There are even presets for the photo apps, for example, in Lightroom, that you can buy for your type of photographs. For example, travel bloggers have pleasing pictures with a certain look and aesthetic feel to them, and that's because they've used these presets to make their pictures look consistently beautiful. These apps enhance what you see, and make it look like what you saw in real life. Best of all, these apps are really easy to use and take just a few seconds to get the best quality picture you can.

It's also a good idea to take just a few classes on photography and videography to learn the best way to frame a picture, compose a scene, etc. Videos can't be quickly edited and improved with apps, so it's important to understand basics like lighting. For example, there are certain gyms that I go to, based on the lighting, for photos to post on Instagram. In our line of work, it's important that we look the best we can. Obviously, in the fitness world, the better you look, the more credibility you have.

When you are taking photos for your Instagram, these are the types of details you want to think about. Where's the best place to take the picture? What's in the background? Is it neat or crowded? How's the lighting? What's the composition of the photo? Is it pleasing? Is it showing what you want it to show?

When you get a chance, take a look at my Instagram feed and compare photos from 4-5 years ago to what I post now. I think you'll see a big improvement. I'm not bragging here, it's just a matter of fact. By taking the time to learn some basic techniques and basics, your photographs will naturally improve and attract more followers. That with meaningful content attached, and thoughtful captions will make those posts look their best. With that quality, I noticed more engagement with my followers, which puts you the algorithm for trending pages, which gets you more connections and more followers.

Again, it comes down to putting out quality content. Photos count as content on Instagram, for sure. So, putting time and thought into your content, including photos, is a great way to grow your Instagram feed. The retention rate of your followers tends to be higher when you put out photos and content.

As people are scrolling through Instagram, image (literally) is everything. When you put yourself out there, your image is what people are looking at. Having high-quality content, including photos and videos puts your best you out there. It screams "success" and "expertise." If your Instagram feed reflects these points, they're hooked. Someone who follows me because they want to get more fit is looking to me because I have achieved that. Again, this is not to brag, but just to point out what people are looking for. If you've got expertise on a subject, and someone follows you on Instagram, it's because you are where they want to be.

This doesn't mean you have to do a professional photo shoot four times a week. Again, utilize what you have. I've done the professional photo shoots, and they don't do as well as natural, more spontaneous photos, and videos. I've noticed that a high-quality selfie in a mirror will do more for my Instagram success than a professional, staged photograph, for example. Images have to be sharp, and not blurry. Lighting has to be just right to show off what I'm trying to emphasize.

Another thing that I've learned, at least in the fitness world, is the vast majority of my photographs are natural, high quality, instead of professional shoots, so people get to see what I really look like. So often when I go to a fitness convention, fans will say, "Wow, you look just as good, if not better, than you do on your Instagram page." So often people are disappointed when they meet someone who has professional, polished and airbrushed images only on their feeds. People meet them in person and wonder who it is that they're seeing right in front of them.

Casual photographs make me seem more human and approachable because I am. I think this encourages raving fans because they're not as likely to jump from person to person, or page to page. If they've met me and they see I look like I say I look, and how I show myself on Instagram, there's a sense of honesty and authenticity that is valuable to them.

Another way to think about this is how you are demonstrating that you care about your content and are committed to helping people. If your photos are of low quality, blurry and have no real value, it shows people that you really don't care. On the other hand, if your photos are high quality, and it's obvious that you've put some time and effort into your videos, people will care and connect, because they know that you care, too. That commitment is really great for business.

In your captions and descriptions, make sure you are always using proper grammar and spelling, punctuation and phrasing. That reflects on how much you care. You want to make sure that you are treating your social media accounts like a full-time job if you ever plan on monetizing your platform.

If you are trying to record your progress on anything, be it fitness, or your handiwork, or even how well you play the ukulele, don't forget to document your "before" photos and videos. Hey, we are all learning, and improving, and getting better at what we do. Be that inspiration that shows people that you weren't born with that body, or with that knowledge, or with that talent. Show your progress, so they know that they can make progress, too.

Let's say you want to lose forty pounds and you want to share what you learn with others. Take that picture of yourself when you look and feel your worst. Even if you don't post it, you still have it. A year or two from now, when you can show off your sleek new body, you can have that before picture to document how far you've come. The best way to help a person is to bridge the gap from where they are to where they want to be. How you motivate them is by showing them you've walked the same bridge.

And, this process continues. Even today, I know that as I continue to get better and learn more about how to improve my own self, the pictures that I take now are going to be another set of "before" pictures. This is a constant cycle that we all have to acknowledge and act on. If you're committed to improvement in everything you do, you'll surprise yourself with how much you continue to improve, and you'll be more relatable to your fans.

It's too hard sometimes to see your own transitions and transformations. You know how it is. You see someone that you haven't spent time with for a few years, and they're really gotten in shape, or improved their health, and you can hardly believe it's the same person. They, on the other hand, might not see that in themselves. I remember looking at a picture of a friend who was in an unhappy relationship, but five years later, now that he was out of the relationship, he looked 10 years younger than when that picture was taken. So, don't be afraid of those "before" pictures. Let your audience see and appreciate your efforts so that they can see that they can do it, too. Take a photo that makes you feel uncomfortable.

Homework

Take a look at the Instagram pages you follow and visit often. What do you notice about their photographs? Chances are, they are high-quality pictures. Take a look at a few of those pages and see if you notice any other patterns in their photographs. Note what you find here:

_____

_____

_____

_____

_____

_____

_____

_____

_____

_____

_____

_____

_____

_____

_____

_____

_____

"Get comfortable with being uncomfortable."

Chapter 4

Post with a Purpose

If you want to get the right content and get it out there, you have to really think about it before you post anything. There are so many people who just slap things up there, and post nonsense, and that will not gain any sort of influence or engagement. 90-95% of your content should be posts that matter, and posts that have a specific meaning or intention.

Your intentions and purpose can be different. Maybe you want to post to entertain. Maybe you want to put something up to inform, motivate or educate. Often, this comes down to the caption. The picture might be worth a thousand words, but the caption is what defines your purpose. It's really easy to either overthink or under-think captions, especially when you're first getting started. There is definitely a fine line between writing too much, and not writing enough.

But you do want to make sure that it is very clear that the purpose and even the timing of your post is deliberate.

Every post has a purpose, even if that means just showing your humanity. Again, 90-95% of your posts should match the purpose and interest of your audience and fan base. The format of your posts should have a purpose, too. For example, I will post 2-3 photos, then a video. The timing, too, is pretty critical. If I have something to sell, I want to build up with many posts and give away a lot of content before I ask for a purchase.

A post should fit into one of the following categories: inspire, entertain, humor, motivate, take action, inform, and promote. These principles are an accumulation of what we have been studying for years.

To inspire someone, ask yourself: who inspires you? Ask yourself WHY do they inspire you? Anyone who helps motivate you to be the best version of yourself to be is going to be an inspiration. This is often done through personal stories and extracting lessons from personal experiences. These inspirers deliver a solution to a problem that you have. They're relatable. They take action daily by doing things sometimes no one else wants to do (even though you know you should do them).

Can you create that persona on your Instagram feed? Can you inspire someone to get to where they want to be? You can if you make sure your posts follow that model. Does your post tell an inspiring personal story? Does it teach through experience? Does it solve a problem? Is your Instagram personality human and relatable? Are you walking the walk and taking the action that your followers need to take?

Always, when you think about how to build your own Instagram following, go back to the pages that you follow and visit often. My guess is that you'll notice that your favorite pages have a variety of posts. In other words, they're not all just informative or motivating, or entertaining, or funny. The pages that you visit often, and find yourself being motivated by, tend to be the ones that tap into a wide variety of posts that help you achieve what you are looking for from that type of page. I think that to get the most out of your Instagram feed, especially if you want to monetize your page, you should find a good balance between all of these post categories.

The humor on my page is a natural humor. In other words, I don't post jokes or overt and obvious humor. But, when telling my story, I can insert natural humor or crack a self-deprecating remark. I think this goes a long way to humanizing me to my fans and increases relatability. Raving fans will watch those stories, and they become even more of a raving fan. It's a simple way to connect without seeming or feeling forced, because it isn't. That's the beauty of the story format. Your dedicated fans will follow those stories, and maybe share with other potential followers, either directly via their internet connections, or while chatting things up at the gum.

Let's talk about timing and how important it is to consider what time and what day of the week you're posting. The analytics that are built into Instagram help refine this for my pages. The majority of our followers are in the United States, so I post based on that. But, it's a little bit more fine-tuned than that. For example, if I'm going to post a recipe, I might do it when I think people are more likely to be hungry like lunch time, or before late-night cravings. Posting a workout in the middle of the day isn't as helpful as posting that in the morning or early evening when people are more likely to be working out. Maybe first thing in the morning would be a good time to post something that's motivating.

I actually think that paying attention to time also increases relatability. It shows a basic understanding of where most people are in their day, and also recognizing what most people do during the day. If I post something midday about great lunch options or short workouts that can be done during a work-day, it's recognizing and acknowledging that most people have a set work schedule, a set lunch hour, and they can use some help and motivation during the workday.

When it comes to days of the week or specific days, there are some basics to follow here, as well. It's not wise to post when millions of eyes are on their televisions, and not on their phones, during the Super Bowl game, for example.

Posting on holidays is another time when your engagement will be low because people are spending time with their families. Date nights like Friday and Saturday nights, people just aren't on their phones as often, so you don't want to do a launch of a product on a Saturday night. Save the good content for a great time.

At the same time, think about the content's focus. What is the point of this post? Where does this post fall in the day? If the point of this post is to sell protein through a recipe, maybe I should post around noon because people are going to be on their phone, they're going to be on their lunch break, and they're likely to buy. Or, it's Friday, it's payday, today might be a good day to launch a new product. You just want to make sure that what you're posting times make sense.

I love Transformation Tuesdays, where I get to show my transformation. I think this can be really motivating. Wisdom Wednesdays to share and educate. These "designated" days keep and maintain a certain rhythm of posts that people almost look for now. This sometimes also gives me a chance to use old content that was good, but that I wasn't able to post at the moment. For example, posting during a convention is great, but Flashback Friday's I can post something that I didn't have time for, or, it just didn't fit what the theme was when I was actively posting during the convention.

One way to think of your Instagram feed is as a billboard for your brand. If I am posting with a purpose, I am thinking of that branding, and what it is I'm ultimately trying to do. In my efforts to post things that are helpful to people, and improving their lives, while finding ways to monetize that, I have to keep that in mind every time I post. It takes years and years and years to build up that brand and image. It doesn't happen just because you build a website, or start offering a service, or put your name on something. That reputation that you establish as a leader in your field takes time, and there are no shortcuts. I know, for instance, people follow my feed because they want some tips and ideas on how to get and stay healthy.

That doesn't mean I can't overlap personal moments with that message. For example, if I post a picture of me out with my friends at dinner, I might caption it something like, "Out with my friends for dinner. If you want some tips and hints on how to eat healthy when dining out, click here!" Or, here I am on a road trip, here's a selfie of us at the gas station, and here's a way you can eat healthy at a truck stop. These bring a human quality to your Instagram feed, make it fun for you to post, but also maintain that purpose and messaging.

If I post that Josh and I post a picture of us going out with friends, and they're all drinking, I might reinforce our commitment to health by saying, "Hey, we went out with some friends, and they're drinking, but here are our strategies to not drink when going out with friends, and still have a great time." Sometimes that takes some thought to remember to post tips like that because it's just habitual for us, and we don't think to talk about that. For example, if we are in a situation where we have to grab a fast food meal, we ditch the bun and the cheese. That's a great tip for people to know if they want to stay fit, but sometimes have to resort to fast food when traveling, or on those really busy days. So, when I'm trying to relate to my followers, I'm trying to relate to them in a way that can be helpful. I don't want to relate to their bad habits without offering a solution or option that maybe they didn't consider.

Homework

What are some things that you do on a daily basis that you take for granted, that some other people might not even think to do, and that might be helpful? For example, here are some tips I've shared with people:

If I have a fitness class early in the morning, I sleep in my workout clothes, so all I have to do is throw on my shoes, and I'm out the door.

Josh dips his fork in his salad dressing and then takes a bite of the salad. He uses about 5% of the salad dressing that he normally would.

Set your alarm clock so that it's across the room so you have to get out of bed to shut it off.

"If you want a million fans, you have to shake a million hands."

Chapter 5

Engage with Everyone

Instagram makes it so easy to engage with other people. For example, just the simple act of liking someone's comment, or responding with a "heart." This little effort goes a long, long way. I get so many screenshots of someone posting and tagging me @sarah_bowmar, saying "She liked my comment!" Again, this is such a simple thing to do, and it goes so far, because I think it shows that you really care. If you want people to engage with you, then you need to be engaging with them.

If you want a million fans, you need to shake a million hands. Let's take a look at what a handshake means. Sure, when I go to conferences or gatherings, and I meet people and shake their hands, that counts. But, with social media, it makes it easier to do this. On Instagram, a handshake is virtual, but it still feels personal. Just like when you meet someone, and you look them in the eye and introduce yourself, that same feeling can be achieved on a social media platform like Instagram. A "handshake" is a comment back, a response to a DM, a "like." You have to give as many virtual handshakes as you can. When you are first starting out, especially, make it really personal.

One quick way to do this is if someone comments on your post, click on their Instagram name, which is usually not their real name, and you'll see their real name come up. Maybe their Instagram name is @fitinaz98, but when you click on that name, you'll see that their real name is David Jones. So, when you comment back, include that name, like, "Hi David, thanks so much for your comment..." This shows that little extra effort. This will show your fans that you actually really do care- any extra effort goes so far.

Engaging can come in other ways, too. For example, we get dozens of tags to our Bowmar Nutrition page in fans' personal stories. When they tag us, I reciprocate by featuring them in our story. Right away, most of the time, that fan will then post how excited they were to be featured by Bowmar Nutrition, and how much it meant to them. That level of engagement can't be bought. It's a chain reaction of you caring and taking the effort for one person, and that person letting their entire social network know how you've helped them. It's the 21st-century version of "word-of-mouth" advertising.

It's a rippling effect. Once you engage with a person, it entices them to tag you more and engage more. People go crazy over this, and I would, too. Then their friends see that, and they're more likely to comment back.

If a fan and customer is going to take the time to tag our product on their page, we are 100% going to take the time to thank them with a return comment like, "Thanks so much for posting Bowmar Nutrition." We have several stock responses that we use. The bottom line is you're making an effort, you're taking extra time to thank someone, and you're shaking their hand.

I am so grateful that people tag our products. I would rather spend five hours a day responding to tags than just about any other "marketing" effort. Because, it's so personal, and it's so effective. It's really an attitude of gratitude. A lot of people lose this the more popular they get. They forget that this isn't a chore. Yes, you have to treat it like a job, but don't lose the mindset that these people who are tagging you are going out of their way to show the love toward your product, and toward your efforts. They are giving you money that they work hard for. They are doing that because they trust the product, and they enjoy the content that I'm putting out there.

Sure, now we have the reviews of our great tasting supplements, but before we had those, before anyone had ever tried any of the nutrition products, people had to trust us with their hard-earned money. That just amazes me that people would do that, and I can never, ever forget that feeling, and take advantage of that. People can sniff insincerity a mile away, so any comments or responses have to be made with the heart, and with that send of appreciation that remembers the feeling of that first purchase and absolute trust of what we were trying to do. Especially since the supplement industry is overcrowded, with so many bad products out there, that when people trusted us and our products, it's humbling. I have never lost that gratitude. And, that's what I try to communicate when I take 4-5 hours each day to thank people for trusting us.

Everyone that follows you is a real person. They are not just a tag on Instagram. There's an actual person behind that tag, or post, or comment. They are taking the time to comment about you, taking the time to tag you. You have to give them the time to comment back, or tag back. If you always remember that those are real people, it will change the whole way you look at your page. Trust is not just about posting, but it's about showing up, even on those days you don't want to. And showing up is the same thing as being like that local business that's always there, that's always available.

That level of trust doesn't happen in a week, or a month, or even a year. It can take years to achieve. But, once it's there, it's your responsibility to maintain it. You have to show up every day for weeks, months, years. If you have the opportunity to be at an expo or convention, be one the first people there, and one of the last to leave. You are showing up in a way that makes it feel very personal, and very human.

You are not just making an appearance. You are reaching out, human to human, and being grateful and gracious. A mistake that I see a lot of would-be influencers make is the, "Hey, I'll be at this booth from 12:00-2:00 on Saturday." Really, you only have two hours for your fans? Last year we were at an expo, we spent 12 straight hours, meeting people who were standing in line to see us. It's only one weekend a year, it's the least I can do to show my appreciation for these people who believe in me and what I do. If you have an opportunity to work with a company at an expo, or just go to an expo, and meet with people in person, it goes far beyond the reach that your social media has. And it is humanizing. The most common comment I get is how short I am! The other really common comment is how "real" we are. That's part of making that human connection that we all crave and need.

A personal pet-peeve of mine is when a fitness personality keeps a really long arm's length from their fans. Maybe they only show up for that short appearance, or you can only get your picture taken with them if you buy a product. We set up our own booth, because we love that aspect of remembering where we've come. It's so satisfying setting out our own booth at The Arnold, the biggest fitness convention of the year, and we absolutely love meeting everyone.

I'm sure that by time this book is published, that the Instagram algorithm will change, but for now- keep this in mind. To register the algorithm, a comment only counts if it's longer than four words. Your posts have to engage in a way that is asking a question, or starting a conversation, that will result in a meaningful comment. Ask, "Hey, do you guys like these workouts?," "What kind of blog post should I write next?, "or "What kinds of recipes are you interested in?" Post things that make people want to engage with you. The same goes for your comments back, too. Make them meaningful and as a way to further connect.

The first 10 minutes of any post are the most important, too. When you post, you want to make sure that you can be online for at least 10 minutes so you can comment back. "Thank you so much for the like (or comment)," "I'm so glad you love this workout," or "So glad you like the recipe. Enjoy!" This timing, and the word-length, affect whether or not you get exposure on the "Popular Pages" or not.

A side note...we want our pages to feel positive and safe. So, we do filter and delete comments that feel weird, or that are negative or insulting. There's really no place for that, so we keep track of things pretty carefully.

Homework

What are you currently doing when it comes to engaging with your target audience?

How are you engaging with people that you look up to?

How much time each day do you currently set aside to engage with your audience? (I personally don't go to bed with an unanswered DM)

_____

_____

_____

_____

_____

_____

_____

_____

_____

_____

_____

_____

"If you can identify someone's problem better than they can, you are automatically accredited the solution."

Chapter 6

Try Not to Outsource

A lot of companies or entrepreneurial individuals hire agencies to write their content or post their photos- and you can always tell. Not in a good way, either. In some ways, I get it. Sometimes I want to outsource, because it would free up time. In some ways it would be awesome because that gives me more time to be creative. I could develop more recipes, or think of new ways to add to a workout routine. That's what I do best.

But, here's what I've found. Anytime anyone ever makes that transition to outsourcing, people can tell, and it's no longer the page that it was. You end up losing the followers that you gained in the first place, leading to a downward spiral to failure. Now, if we got up to 100 million followers, would we need help? Yes, absolutely. But, both Josh and I are committed to never disengaging with our followers. Ever.

Everyone's workload is different. You have to factor in what you can realistically do, so if you have to hire help for running your website, or anything else, maybe pick tasks that don't involve direct contact with your followers. Or, if you have to do that, you have to maintain direct oversight, and I mean checking things over, every day. Delegation is not a bad thing, if you do it right. The bottom line is that you can delegate tasks, but not responsibility. You have the ultimate responsibility to set the tone of your page, to communicate with fans effectively and sincerely. If you disconnect from this part of the process, you will ultimately disconnect from your fans and followers, and you will ultimately fail.

Another good reason to stay on top of responding to comments and DMs yourself is how it can actually shape the conversations that you have on your page. For example, if I am reviewing all the comments, and responding to them, I can start to see patterns of common questions, and inquiries. I can then write blogs related to what I'm seeing on the page, and then refer people to that blog post when it comes up. I can dedicate time to writing a well thought out blog post, so people have a clear and concise answer. Or, I can post a video that answers common questions. That, in turn, increases engagement with page followers, and personalizes their experience.

My blog provides Instagram page followers another space to go to. For example, I have more than 4 million hits on my blog because of the additional information and resources that are available there. Also, since Instagram has IGTV, you can record 10 minute videos explaining a question. It's quick, and you can send people a link to the video. I think that answering your own comments and DMs not only increases that personal touch, you can base what you learn by the questions on how you can add content and valuable information to your website, Instagram feed, or blog. Clearly, if people are asking, it's because you're not providing that type of content. So, listen, learn and find where you need to focus your attentions, based on what people are asking you.

I don't mind at all if someone asks a quick question that maybe I posted a blog on a while back. Sure, they could spend half a day searching for a specific post, but people, in general, don't have time to do that. Even if the information IS on the Instagram page, or blog, or website, or wherever, I don't mind sending a link. It's not THEIR job to research my website. It's my job to connect and communicate and develop content that is helpful.

To keep this personal touch, and avoid outsourcing, especially as your fan base grows, you have to create systems. The scalability after 100,000 followers is really hard.

When you get to a half million or a million, you're talking about a couple of hundred DMs a day. It can get a little overwhelming and time consuming. If you put it in perspective of a 9 to 5 job, you don't even think about putting in that time. You have to treat your Instagram page as a full time job and allocate that time to it. Otherwise, if you don't treat it as a full-time job or a full-time business, it won't pay you as a full-time business.

We run six instagram pages. Two personal accounts, two supplement companies, our cat page (LOL) and then our outdoor page. Between them all, I can easily spend 3-5 hours per day responding to comments, developing content, responding to DMs, and that doesn't include the time necessarily filming and editing videos, etc.

Make sure you have the systems in place so that you're not answering the same questions over and over, start a blog to be an additional resource for your followers. If you have a gmail account, they have a great blogging system called Blogger (it's FREE). You can write your own blog and use it to give people a place to go to if they're asking the same questions that have already been asked before. You can cultivate your content around things that people are asking. In these blog posts, I can also plug our own products or products that I believe in. We limit direct selling in our content, because we want to build those relationships. A decent formula that we follow is 3-4 high quality content pieces before we mention a product or service that we sell, or even just ask someone to do something, like go to a website, or blog, or use a discount code.

A lot of people ask me if it's worth outsourcing the scheduling of posts. In other words, I can write a post at 7 in the morning but have it scheduled to post at noon. I highly discourage this. In order to "schedule" a post, you are giving a third-party app your sign-in information, and I've seen a lot of people have their accounts compromised this way. More importantly, though, is that we talk in this book about how important it is to reply to comments within the first 10 minutes of a post. You lose that ability when you are scheduling a post. We've had times where we've gone to Alaska, for example, and have posted that we're off the grid and there won't be any posts for a week. Now, if the page keeps posting, people will know that those posts are scheduled, and that can somewhat discredit your authenticity.

When we were first building our Instagram pages, YouTube channels, and everything else related to our businesses, we did EVERYTHING. From accounting, to graphic design to editing. I think it's so important to do that, so that you know what it involves, how to get what you are expecting, and to communicate to people that you might outsource some of these tasks to. If you do outsource some tasks, make sure you know the ins and outs of that task, and know how to communicate exactly what you need. If you outsource, don't do it too quickly. I think that's a huge mistake. That can sometimes mean you'll get taken advantage of, and you won't be able to communicate properly with the person who's doing the task for you. You may not understand time-frames, or realistic expectations, or all the nitty gritty details of things, so you'll be able to keep employees because you'll be a better supervisor and leader. By doing this, you're all on the same page, and you can create extraordinary things together.

As you build your business and your brand and your image, you may find you need to outsource. It's not a terrible thing, but don't beat yourself up if your production values aren't as slick or polished as someone who's been doing this for years. So, don't rush into outsourcing, be yourself, be human, learn and continue to improve. Outsource only when it gets really overwhelming, and day to day tasks are taking you away from your creative side. Everything that you need to do to build a large social media following is skill based, not talent based. Every skill can be learned.

Homework

What is a common trend of things that people are saying or commenting on your page? If you don't have your own page set up yet, go to a favorite Instagram page of yours and look over common themes.

What are some that you see?

1.

2.

3.

4.

5.

Tally those types and categories for a week or two to see what you might notice about how to calibrate your content based on those comment themes.

"Your vibe attracts your tribe"

Chapter 7

Strategic Ways to Gain Followers

When I first started growing my page, I followed a few women who had a similar following as me, and who had similar interests. We would post each other to gain followers for each account and then take those posts down. I'm not sure if this would be as effective in today's Instagram algorithm, and it does change all the time, but story shout-outs or post shout-outs are really effective. When you're doing a shout-out it's important to keep in mind that a lot of people say they don't want to pay for a shout-out. But, if you work together with someone, you can put this to your advantage.

Basically, a shout-out can be a sharing of stories, or of posts. I find that videos do really well on shout-outs if it's a fitness page. If you can post someone else's workout, for example, and say something like, "Here's a great workout, with other good information like what you see on our page." I work with other pages so we can help build up our followers, so I'll send a DM or email, or even a message via WhatsApp, to let them know I've posted a shout-out for their page, and send one that they can add to their page, complete with caption, link, etc. A shout for shout is very common, and then after an hour, or two, or even 24 hours, you delete that post, and they delete the post you sent. That way the personality of your page stays intact, and you've both gained followers.

Let's say I have five hundred followers, and I find someone who has 500 followers in the same category. I then create a post with a shout-out for that other page. If I post a shout-out from a business or person in a completely different category, it can really hurt my algorithm and page standings. For example, if I post a shout-out for a Truck Page on my page, my fans and followers aren't going to be interested, and they'll scroll right by. The more a fan scrolls past your content, the less Instagram will show your page to that person. Why show them a page that they clearly don't engage with or like?

Shout-outs have to be engaging, and if they're not, your posts will be scrolled past and you'll be put into an algorithm that your followers will see less and less of your posts and content. The increase in engagement can increase your followers, and the next thing you know, you're at 5,000 followers. Then you're at 100,000 and the exponential growth continues. Now, there are shortcuts, where you can pay big bucks to do that, but really you can grow it organically. Instead of paying someone with 100,000 followers, when you have 5,000, to do a shout-out, you can grow with other people at the same time.

There's nothing wrong by paying someone to do a shout-out of you, when it's in the same category. Right now, the price is really very inexpensive, because the bigger companies haven't gotten into it. I suspect that when they do (not, if...but, WHEN), the price will be astronomical. Take advantage of this opportunity, while it's still affordable. Instagram also allows you to sponsor yourself, so if you want to pay to reach more potential followers in a certain market, you do it in Facebook Ad Manager, and you can pay to promote yourself, or your company to people. Again, this is a feasible option, but about three times as expensive if you were to pay someone else to do a shout-out for you and reach way more people.

As an example, if you wanted to pay to reach 200,000 people, you would probably pay Instagram $1,500-2,000. But, if you were to pay someone else to reach their 200,000 followers, it might only cost about $80-100. These are ballpark numbers, and I'm sure that by time you read this, those figures will have changed, but the core truth that it's less expensive to pay for a shout-out will most likely stand.

Another great way to gain followers is by finding other influencers in your similar field. Go to their following and like their posts, most people do have their notifications turned on so when they get a like- they see it immediately. This may prompt someone to check your page out and follow you as long as your content is something worth following. This will take a lot of effort and work, but it can be a very effective way to grow a following.

Liking photos and engaging with other popular Instagram personalities, in your same niche, will increase your exposure as well. The last two comments on any photo that someone with a big following posts are either someone that you're following, or someone with a big following. Even if those comments aren't the most recent ones, they're always as the bottom. So, it's always worthwhile to engage with others who have a large following, because your name and your comment will show under their photo. Remember, you always want to be authentic. You don't want to comment and slap some emojis on there just to comment. This is also a way to engage with someone who does have a large following, and you can build a relationship with them just because of that comment. We've actually become friends with some well-known Instagram personalities due to this.

Even if it feels like some of these tricks feel a little like cheating, it doesn't matter if, at the end of the day, you're posting quality content and information. That's what people appreciate the most. In other words, if you're trying to gain followers for the right reasons, I don't think it's a bad thing of how you gain a follower, as long as you're trying to make the world a better place. Josh's brother liked posts and gained over 23,000 followers, just by doing that. He treated it like a job and did it every day. People like to think it's just going to take one viral post, and they'll gain all these followers. It doesn't work that way for the vast majority of us. Sure, if The Rock posts you, you might get 30,000 followers in an hour. But, don't count on it. Just buckle down and do the work.

I think if you really put in the work and take the time and effort to get followers and provide high quality content, you can gain a substantial Instagram page in about a year. That may seem like a long time, but that amount of time is going to pass whether or not you do the work. At the end of the year, do you want to be just where you are today, in regards to Instagram followers, or fitness goals, or saving up for your dream vacation? Or, do you want to see how much further you can be in a year. Set aside a half-hour each day, at least, to work on growing your following, in addition to the time you spend creating and posting content.

You could easily reach 0-10,000 followers in 30-60 days if you do this, IF you have the content to back it up. Content FIRST! You need to have at least 50-60 posts, up and rolling, before you can expect any followers. Why?

That's three scrolls and someone will be able to judge your content off three scrolls.

You'll never get there, however, if you don't post enough high-quality content. Count on at least two posts per day. For fitness, maybe a recipe a day, and a workout each day. If you only post sporadically, you won't have the engagement that you need to spark the Instagram algorithm, much less your followers, and they'll drift away.

Homework

To get to that first 10k, or whatever your next follower goal is, set aside 30 minutes a day for a month and see what happens. Liking photos and comments of followers on another similar page, for example. Make sure it's a follower that probably has their notifications on so they see that you've liked something - someone with maybe 1,000-2,000 followers.

List five people to follow that have similar pages:

1.

2.

3.

4.

5.

List five of your favorite hashtags to follow and "like" comments or photos:

1.

2.

3.

4.

5.

Record your progress here:

Starting followers:_____

30-Day Follower Count:_____

What practice did you find the most effective?

_____

_____

Least effective?

_____

_____

"Never water yourself down just because someone can't handle you at 100 proof"

Chapter 8

Creating a Raving Fan

There is nothing more valuable, when it comes to Instagram followers, than a raving fan. I don't mean this in a demeaning way, at all. The people who we identify as raving fans are so appreciated. Not just for their support of us and our businesses, but for their energy and how they keep conversations going in such a positive way. This touches on the importance of being human, which I talk about in another chapter, but it's worth bringing up here in the context of a raving fan.

We hear it all the time when we meet people at conventions and expos, "You are just so real." I think it also comes with being more casual when it comes to photo shoots, for example, because you see a "normal" human being. This type of authenticity is what helps you relate to followers and fans and develops a raving fan base.

What is a raving fan? I'm certainly a raving fan of certain personalities and products. These are people who inspire me, people who help and motivate me, either directly or indirectly. Someone who can provide this sort of inspiration, beyond the content of their Instagram page or website, when you come down to it, is the most helpful. To achieve that level of helpfulness and influence, the importance of relatability has to be emphasized.

Relatability comes from addressing a common problem and providing a solution for someone who may not have known how to move forward without your help. Sure, they might know the basics, but by providing specific ideas, tips, solutions, plans and activities that can help someone solve a problem in their lives, you can be that influencer. That person is looking in the mirror, and they're not liking what they see. Whether it is a physical, emotional or social "reality" that they are looking at. If I can help them get to where they want to be, and like what they see in the mirror, and I do it for free....I've got a raving fan. If you can bridge that gap from where they are now, to where they want to be. If you can give them hope by saying, "Hey, I want to help you," and you share helpful tips that will give them started, you will gain a raving fan. This can translate into monetary value when they are ready for a full program based on the results they have experienced from your free tips.

But, why create a raving fan by giving your services and information away? Raving fans will buy from you. I think the biggest problem that most people have is that they charge for that gap to be bridged. They charge for the information that they could be giving away for free, so they don't get a raving fan. They "maybe" get a fan. Once that fan gives up a dollar of their hard-earned money, their expectations go through the roof, because they're paying for it.

It's always hard to meet people's' expectations, so whenever you don't charge for information, you exceed their expectations 90% of the time. If you can give them a little piece of advice, or help, they will remember that, and that they didn't have to pay for that help.

We have several ways that we make money, through different services and products that we sell. We have them in our Instagram bio, they're sometimes linked in our stories by linking our supplements or services, but I would say that 90-95% of our content has no mention of what we provide. For example, we sell meal plans because we're fitness and nutrition specialists. So, we won't give away the meal plan, but we'll give away diet tips and nutrition information. After a while, someone may write and say, "Oh, by the way, can your write me a meal plan," or we might say something like, "Hey, if you don't want the headache of putting together a meal plan, we can do that for you..." Even if they don't purchase a meal plan, for example, they'll buy something else from us, because we helped them so much with the free information and content.

This is a philosophy and approached that we've transitioned into. Most people ignore their critics, but by paying attention if there's one person "hating" on one subject, there are probably 100 thinking the same thing, but not saying anything. Sarcastic comments like "you couldn't post any more discount codes if you tried", is a clue that you are asking too much. Your formula might be off.

When you are "giving away" so much information, for so long, when you finally ask for a purchase, or attach a link, you're now entitled to do that. In fact, your raving fans are going to feel almost obligated to throw something your way, because they appreciate your effort, and sincerely want to support you. If you try to fast-track leaving your full-time job to make money off of your page, and you appear as desperate to sell things and make money, you'll turn off any potential raving fan. All of this takes time to develop. You won't have an influence over people, and fans that you don't have influence over will not buy something from you. This creates a downward spiral, where you're not truly engaging in a way that creates a raving fan, you're going to fail.

One way to know if you're doing this right is to notice that the time you spend engaging with followers is going up, as your followers go up. If that's not happening, those are not followers or fans that are going to help you earn money from your Instagram feed. You maybe don't have any real fans. You might just have people who haven't unfollowed you....yet.

People sometimes ask me who I follow, and who I've been a raving fan of, either in the fitness world or outside of it. I mention people like Gary Vee, Tony Robbins, Steve Cook in the fitness world and someone we like to model. Basically, I like to follow people who have a crazy (in a good way) raving fan base, and model what they do, and their formulas. One of my favorites is Amanda Latona, a fitness expert who models sincerity and appreciation of her fans, commitment to her husband and family, and staying true to herself and not changing despite her popularity.

Most people aren't students of life. We tend to think education only means getting through high school or college. If you want to ruin any potential for success, you should keep that mentality that your learning is over. Be a good student and study people that you love and appreciate. Even if you don't like them, but they have a raving fan base, they're doing something right. Pay attention! Learn basic business and sales strategies to have the best chance of success.

To create a raving fan base, make sure you are offering great content for free, AND have something of quality to sell. That's part of having a raving fan base; being able to help someone with something that general information is just not going to do. Whatever you're selling, it needs to enhance their life. That's why we created the supplements we have. That's why we offer the custom services that we do. That's why we spend money on developing these things, learning and getting certified to offer great services to our fans, we invest money that we receive into continued improvement and offerings.

When you ask for a sale, you need to be very, VERY careful about which product and service that you are actually asking money for. Because you can only do this so many times. Make sure you give this some real thought, because a lot of people don't. They might get one sponsor and then two sponsors, then ten sponsors, and the next thing you know every other post is, "Hey, use my coupon code." Only work with companies that you are a raving fan and genuinely love their products and/or services. Nothing is more annoying to a fan that being sold something that they don't think you believe in.

Think about every sponsorship as an investment. A sponsor will work with you because they have an expectation that you will sell for them. For example, if a sponsor gives you $300, they expect you to "sell" $900 of product. How many times do you have to post so that you can sell that product? How many posts would you need to have to sell that much? Is it worth it to you? Is it worth the $300 that is being offered? If you think through every sponsorship this way, you'll find that some are worth it to you, and many are not. If you take every sponsor that comes your way, your page just turns into an advertising platform for your sponsors.

There are different levels of sponsorship, many start off with a discount code to buy your own product, then free product, then a discount code or commission link, and then a salary and free product. This is why it is vital to be a raving fan of a company prior to a sponsorship offer. Selling a product or talking about a brand you actually love, and use is so effortless when you truly believe it will help someone else. Trying to sell a product you don't believe in, comes across ingenuine and unauthentic. Doing this too many times will result in you appearing ingenuine without your followers best interest at heart.

If you have to switch companies, explain to your fans as to why - maybe there was a restructuring, maybe you noticed there was a much better product that you wanted to throw your efforts behind. Don't bash the old sponsor, just talk about the positive reasons you might have changed sponsors. This establishes trust between you and your raving fans and shows that you are a professional to your current and potential future sponsors. Just be authentic, and honest. That's your best sales tactic, and it is in keeping with what we try to do, always. The joke we make is to do the opposite of what you really want to say, then you'll be ok. Take the high road.

Homework

Take a look, again, at your favorite influencers on Instagram, but this time with an eye on their sponsorships, and the things that they may sell. What do you notice about:

1. The ratio of quality free content to sales asks?

2. The type of sponsorships, and how many they carry?

3. Whether or not you've purchased something from them.

4. The relationships they have with some of their key sponsors?

"The main thing in life is to not be afraid of being human"

SARAH & JOSH BOWMAR

Chapter 9

Being Human

One of the most important things I think you can do for your Instagram page is to be human. As I've mentioned before, people like people that they can relate to. Instagram makes this easy with the "story" feature, where you can really show more of your humanness and personality, and then it goes away in 24 hours, so you don't lose the focus of your page. The highlight feature is awesome, too, and I hope it's something that Instagram keeps around. For example, I launched a highlight during the end of the previous year, so I can highlight the entire year. Even if it's just for my pleasure, but beyond that, the highlight really gives insight into who I am, and I hope makes me more relatable to our fans and followers. I can also share content there, like recipes, fun stuff, general personal highlights - it just gives people a place to find what they need.

In keeping with the aspect of nurturing a raving fan base, the importance of being human, and relatable, is critical. The story function of Instagram is great for this. These are things that you share on a more human scale; things that you care about. Like family, friends, hobbies, going to out - just hanging out. You can really connect and relate with your fan base in a very real way. For example, as a couple, once a week, we go on a date night, because people look up to us in that way, too. So, we'll document our date night, the food, etc.

In fitness, I think the human side is important to show that you're not "perfect." You go out to eat, you have a piece of cake on your birthday, you sometimes skip the gym so you can sleep in. It's just so important to show that side, because sometimes people don't think of you as a person, especially if you have a certain number of followers. We all deal with "haters" on Instagram and in other social media settings, and if you come off as a superhuman, you're more vulnerable to attacks. When you create a family of raving fans, they'll often jump in and stick up for you, because you've shared with them your human side, including mistakes you make, and things you screw up.

Something that I've found helpful is to think of a raving fan as a friend. When someone meets you, they need to know all the elements that a friend would know about you. We call our raving fans our digital family. I have Instagram friends who

82

know more about my personal life than members of my family. I love it when I go to a festival like the Arnold, and someone will come up to me and remind me about the vacation I took the year before. Or, something like, "Boy, that meal you posted last week looked so good." By knowing these intimate details about us, when they meet us, they know that we're human, that we're vulnerable. Posting things on your stories that show your human and vulnerable side really creates this type of relationship with your followers that will help you achieve whatever your goals are with Instagram.

Raving fans love stories, so you know they're going to go there, and you know they're going to watch it. When you create your Instagram story, and you open up and share a vulnerable side of you, you develop this heartstring that connects you. It's information that you normally wouldn't share with the public. Think of your Instagram story as a private, special place to post certain things that are more vulnerable than others. I think this is the perfect place to admit that you slept in, even if you had made a promise to yourself that you would get up at 5:00 that morning.

There's an interesting dynamic that I should talk about, that you might run into at one point. When I first met Josh, we each had our own following. We brought things together to create a unified fan base, and fans who have grown with us. As we "grow up," our friends grow up with us. Boyfriends turn into husbands, girlfriends into wives. There's almost a mirroring that speaks to the connections we have with our fans. That mutual feeling of being human and establishing a relationship with followers is best grown organically, and it's something that just happens naturally. Because fans have known us as singles, then dating, and now married, we also have a legitimacy as a couple, and people look up to us and our relationship. This shares a very human side between us and our followers, and it's very special.

When you create stories on Instagram, you don't have to worry too much about how pretty or polished they are. Stories can be "lower quality" in a way that really shows that you're not all glitz and polish. They can almost be used as a "blooper" reel, and people really love to see that side of you. Don't we all? Going live is also super important because it actually shows unfiltered you. There's no retakes, there's no editing, there's no filters, there's only you in that very moment. You can really build that human quality as well, because you'll inevitable say a funny word, or say the wrong thing, and you call yourself out on it, and people can really relate to that. I get so many messages thanking me for going live, and they tell me how much they relate to me through the live videos. I recommend at least once a week, because it opens up yourself to criticism, to be judged. Your raving fans will love this. It's not that they love that you screwed up, or say the wrong thing, or do the wrong thing. They love it because you are now vulnerable, and relatable, and real in their eyes.

To go live, there are some things to keep in mind, and things I prefer when we go live. I'll try to go live and then follow-up with a Q&A. For example, I might post that I'm going to go live to talk about supplements, so send me your questions that I can answer them, and if we have time, I'll stay online and do a Q&A with people who are on the live feed. I'll save that live feed and put it on our IGTV channel for future reference. Sometimes when we launch a new product we'll go live. Recipes are really popular live, or just tips on how I mix greens or a quick workout tip.

Instagram gives you many ways to share your humanness, you should take advantage of them all. The more relatable you are to your fans, the more they'll engage with you and the more fun you'll have with your Instafamily.

Homework

Like we've done in other chapters, let's go back to those Instagram feeds that you follow closely. Scroll through their feeds for the last week, and note what you find:

1. How is the person or company humanizing themselves?

2. What do you notice about how their followers interact with them and how it improves or distracts from being relatable?

3. What are some things you can feature on your Instagram page that would humanize you? Hobbies? Activities?

4. Think about a live feed that you can put together in the next week. What would the topic be? The format? How would you promote it before the actual live feed?

5. Post your live feed? How did you do? Can you live with the mistakes you made? Is this something that you can reference for future information for your fans and followers?

*"You **make a living** by what you get; you **make** a life by what you give"*

Chapter 10

How to Get Paid

Chances are, you're reading this book to not only learn how to get 1,000,000 followers but also to earn money using social media platforms, like Instagram. When I first started my Instagram, that wasn't my goal. I love to tell people about my first Instagram post, which was of a cupcake on my 22nd birthday. Clearly, I didn't have a monetary goal with that post!

Most of you are looking to monetize your Instagram account, and wisely so. There are many ways to do so, even if you are just getting started.

First of all, start out with a business page. The Instagram platform for business versus personal pages doesn't look that different to a viewer or page visitor, but the business side of things shows you information you need. For example, follower insights and analytics that can help drive and direct your content. Business page analytics can really help you break down why a post might have been more popular than another post. Was it because of a hashtag? Did you ask a thought-provoking question? You'll get way more information than just the number of likes and comments. Also, if you have 10,000 or more followers, and you're set up as a business page, you can add the swipe-up feature, which is very popular with followers. You can also link your business page to Facebook, which makes things much easier when it comes to not having to update multiple accounts and pages.

When people think of how to monetize their Instagram feed, they most often think of sponsorships. This is a common, and relatively easy way to earn money just by having a lot of followers, but there are some important downfalls to consider.

Sometimes sponsorships are gifts from the sponsor, sometimes it's money that you get paid via discount codes, or percentage of sales from your direct links. Sometimes you can just get paid to post, so a company might ask you to help launch a new service by paying you to post a certain number of times on your story. Sponsorship contracts can be very short term, or for a year, or extended and open-ended. You'll likely start to get offers once you have at least 10,000 followers.

Sponsorships are the quickest and easiest way to make money on your Instagram but use that money wisely. Don't just take that cash and blow it. Use it to invest in your own business to grow and expand services and make more money. If you jump ship too soon and leave your full time job before you've got a solid business plan in place, you become a little desperate for the sponsorship income.

Stay clear of the "reach and grab" trap, where you grab at anything that can pay you. If you do decide to get paid for posting sponsor information, you can find out through Social Blue Book how much your posts are worth, so you don't get taken advantage of.

Low hanging fruit have little value - free shirts - post yourself wearing it. Next thing you know that 3-4 posts of value to one post of sales, is going one to one, and you will lose all your influence and power to sell your own products. Or, they'll just scroll by.

Once you seem desperate, your followers will leave in droves. Instead, save that money to enter into a market for your own business (for example- appearl or exercise bands). These are entry level products and your cost of entry can be just $5,000-$10,000. Look to suppliers like AliBaba for cheap ways to enter certain product lines. Or, write a valuable ebook or guide. Maybe launch a video lesson package, or a set of tools with your logo and name on it. If you invest in yourself, and in additional ways to make money besides sponsorships, it preserves your independence, and sets your page up for long term profitably.

On the other hand, be careful how you move into the manufacturing product realm. Not that long ago we started our own supplement company and made a million mistakes. From never visiting the factory, to not participating in the formula of supplements, to pre-selling product that didn't deliver as promised - really, it was a total disaster. We lost over $45,000, and the business failed within a year. Not only were we financially destroyed for the short-term, as you can imagine this was an extremely stressful endeavor.

We prepared for another year before we launched anything new. We stepped back, and as much as we wanted to launch a product right away, we decided to wait based on the lessons that we had learned from our previous disaster. We worked until it was absolutely perfect and absolutely ready. We didn't pre-sell anything nor did we make mention of anything that we were doing, until we actually launched Protein Hot Chocolate. People just went absolutely crazy over it. Obviously, with any product or service, you want to make it as high quality as you can, but with this product we spent so much time, and put so much effort into perfecting it, people just went absolutely bonkers over it.

Supplements may not be what we recommend for you, if you're in the world of fitness. The profit margins are mediocre unless you price gouge your customers, and you have to order an extremely high number of products to create an inventory. You then need to pay for fulfillment, labels, shipping, and a multitude of other expenses. Clothing is the same way, so again don't jump ahead of yourself. We made all the mistakes that you can make on this, so learn from us. Keep in mind that if you start a company with high overhead like this, you have to begin with at least $50,000 out of the gate with your own money, not to mention the cost to maintain supplies.

Maybe you're tempted to get a loan to finance this new product or line. Don't. If you don't have $50,000 to start a high overhead company like supplements, you're not doing something right...yet. Be patient, and grow, earn and invest slowly and methodically. There are no shortcuts here. You have to have a surplus to absorb the initial loss of funds that you're going to feel, and a loan is just going to bite into your profit margin. Worst-case scenario, if your company fails, your loan does not go away. So, now you're doubly down and out.

Outside of sponsorships, a low cost of entry for people, as I mentioned a little bit before, are ebooks. If you are a photographer, for example, you could create an ebook on how to take photos, how to edit your photos, how to organize photos, and other different tips or tricks. The great thing about ebooks is that it doesn't matter if you sell only 10, or you sell 10,000, your cost of entry is the same, and nominal. It's done, it's over with, you can just sell them and make a profit every time. Services like that are great, especially digital services.

Anything you can sell digitally is great, because your profits will be 100%, and that's really helpful, especially as you're just starting out. Other examples you can consider are recipe books and programs that you create once and sell to as many people as you can. A membership-based website is also very profitable. Basically, anything that can take you out of the equation as far as your time goes, because now you're generating passive income.

You can even take old content and package it into a digital product. For example, I constantly post different recipes for free. I can take those recipes, organize them, and put them into one single ebook and post, "Hey, I know you all love those recipes I post, and they're still always free, but if you want one simple place to have them all, here's an ebook where I organized them for you."

I suggest you start with these types of products and services, the kind that have pretty much 100% profit, as you learn business strategies and what works and what doesn't. Then, you can explore "hard" products like apparel, or supplements, or physical books. Some products lend themselves to drop and ship. In other words, you don't have to order big quantities, for example 1,000s of shirts to sell. There are some apparel companies that can just produce one shirt that you ship out - sure, your profit margin won't be as high, but you'll know what products work, and what don't, so that when you have that extra $50,000 saved to start a small apparel company, you've already tested items out. You'll learn so much about what your fans like, what colors, what sizes, and what styles are the most popular. You're not going to lose money on inventory that doesn't sell. Some companies that offer this service include Vistaprint, Printify, and others.

When it comes to developing products like apparel, or equipment and other items that are part of your brand, check your ego at the door. Most people won't be interested in a shirt with your name on it. They might be interested in a shirt with a fun slogan. For example, for our hunting and outdoor site, we have a t-shirt that says, "Built By Venison." Sometimes what happens is I'll order a hat, or a t-shirt on a service like Vistaprint, and post a picture of me wearing it just kind of casually. If I get a lot of inquiries or comments like, "Cool hat, are you selling it?," that can guide me as to what kind of apparel would sell, and I go ahead and place some orders.

Whether or not you attach your name to your company can sometimes really depend on your actual name. Some names lend themselves to being more marketable than others. In fact, Bowmar Nutrition was not our first choice for our supplement company name. A good friend, Jordan Harbertson (owner of the successful outdoor nutrition company MTNOPS), encouraged us to reconsider. He thought Bowmar Nutrition was a great marketable name. With much resistance, we thought he might just be right. Turns out he was, so thanks Jordan! And that's how Bowmar Nutrition was born.

Through all of this, I guess what I need to emphasize is to always think of the end-goal. Is your ultimate goal to develop a company that you can sell? Is your ultimate goal to build your product empire? Is your goal to sell your name as a royalty? What is your ultimate goal? Figure that out and build your company accordingly. Make every decision with that ultimate goal in place. Whether or not your initial goal is to sell your business, it's a good idea to build your business with that goal in mind. You need to reverse engineer your goal. Start with the end in mind and take it back step by step until you have daily and hourly actions. Success doesn't happen by accident, you need to success on purpose every single day.

Josh and I feel qualified to be writing this book and to be providing this advice because of what we have built online. Nothing in the following paragraph is to boast or brag- it is only to validate our credentials for this book. Josh and I became multi-millionaires in our mid 20's by building five successful companies 100% debt free (our largest being Bowmar Nutrition). At the writing of this book, Bowmar Nutrition is only 11 months old. It took us 6 months to do our first $1,000,000 in sales and now we are averaging over

$1,000,000 per month and our business growth hasn't slowed down- in fact, we project exponential growth for 2019 and beyond. Keep in mind, we never borrowed money from family, friends, or the bank- every cent invested came from our own pockets.

We did this by growing it organically. In fact, we were recognized as one of the fastest growing businesses of 2018 on the Shopify platform. We love that this business was built not just on how we look, but by the product quality, the service, and overall customer experience.

We visit the manufacturer several times each year and spend hours and hours, perfecting the flavors and formulas to bring our customers the best products possible., We don't rush anything, we learned that from previous failures. For example, our Christmas flavor we started developing in June. We prepare for huge events like the Arnold months and months in advance to make sure we have enough of the right product to offer. We always try to figure out how we can be different, and how we can be better. We were the first company to develop the idea of drinking protein drinks hot, like our protein hot chocolate. After we had the idea for the hot chocolate protein, it took a year and a half to develop it and offer it, because we had to use special proteins that had high heat tolerances. Good is not good enough when it comes to products. It has to be perfect.

Bowmar Nutrition is also just one of five companies we own. We also own and operate Bowmar Fitness, Bowmar Bowhunting, Natural Science Creation, and Bowmar Bands. We have built all of these based on the principles outlined in this book.

Services they use:

Shopify

Authorize.net

Paypal

Amazon Pay

Vistaprint

Shipping and fulfillment, shoot for under $3 per order

Outsource shipping

Instagram

YouTube

Homework

Think about your end-goal. What do you want your Instagram page to do for you in:

1 year:

_____

_____

3 years:

_____

_____

5 years:

_____

_____

End-goal time frame, and end-goal:

_____

_____

How will you define what you do now, based on your end-goal? Time to reverse engineer your goal- from year to month to week to day to hour. This will keep you on track to accomplish your goals

"Do something wonderful, people may imitate it"

Chapter 11

Copy Other People

First of all, don't take this chapter title literally. Don't copy verbatim, because people see it, and they'll call you out on it. You want to be an original and you want to create your own voice and your own brand. There's also no need to reinvent the wheel and you can learn a lot about how to achieve success by looking at what other people have done. Pay attention to what other successful people are doing.

For example, if someone you look up to is posting five workouts a week, and two recipes a week, a personal photo once a week, and they're doing personal stories, and live feeds, and they're successful at it, that might be a formula that you want to utilize.

People in your field who are successful have a strategy and a system. It's up to you to dissect what that strategy is. What is it that makes them successful? YouTube channels are another great place to do this exploration. Your influencer might have "monthly favorites," or recipes, or healthy tips. Base your topics and your formula off of what you see as already successful.

Set a schedule and decide what your weekly content is going to look like. You don't have to adhere to this 100%, but if you have that goal, and you work toward that, you'll get close most of the time. It will help you stay on track and make sure that your content is consistent. Take note of your following. Is it growing? Are you engaging more and more with your following? Pay attention to what you're doing and you'll never lose that.

A common mistake that I see is that people build a following based on content, and then as soon as they have the following they want, they stop doing what built that following in the first place. They either start selling too much, or taking on too many sponsorships, or just don't engage as much, or outsource interaction and communication with their followers. Many fitness personalities make this mistake- you need to set the ego aside, stop feeling entitled, and have a more "giving" mentality. If you ever start feeling that you don't need to be helpful anymore, you will lose followers, and you will short-change your goals and potential. When you achieve 1,000,000 followers, you almost want to copy yourself, too. Stick to the plan.

Homework

Develop your posting plan by first identifying 5 types of posts that you will create each week. For example, workouts, recipes, shopping lists, helpful hints, live demos.

1.

2.

3.

4.

5.

Now, determine a schedule of posts, for example:

Each Monday:

Each Tuesday:

Each Wednesday:

Each Thursday:

Each Friday:

Each Weekend:

You don't have to necessarily do it by day of the week, but by times per week (e.g. once a week, twice a week, 4 times a week)

"Be helpful, even if there's no immediate profit in it"

Chapter 12

Create Content People Talk About

If you want to build a following, and most importantly, keep that following, your content has to be interesting. How many times have you followed a page or personality, and just gotten bored with their content? Maybe you haven't unfollowed them, but you're certainly not a raving fan, and you're certainly not engaging with the page anymore. You most definitely won't purchase anything, because they've lost their influence on you, and you're just not interested anymore.

What you post doesn't have to be always on subject, because the entertaining factor is critically important. For example, we get so many likes for our "Date Night" posts. If you get stuck on how to caption something, search on Pinterest or Google for funny or inspirational posts. Let's face it- we all lke people who make us laugh! Playful videos are a lot of fun, and people love them!

Most people would describe me as a serious person. So for me to by silly and funny, it doesn't come easy. For me, that's where the live feeds and story feature come into play, because I can be more relaxed. It's important to incorporate posts that show people a fun, magnetic side of yourself.

There are so many Instagram pages that your followers can tune into, so it's up to you to have a wide variety of posts to keep their interest. A balance of humor and playfulness, as well as just pure entertainment, can really keep people connected and engaged with you.

You know, sometimes the world is a really sad place, so if you can help lighten up someone's day, you are really helping them, too. For example, sometimes when we're in the gym, if Josh is recording a workout, I'll wave in the background. Or, Josh will throw up a flex when he's recording a workout of mine. It always comes back to helping people, and if I can do something on my feed that makes them smile, or laugh, or just brings a little lightness to their day, they'll really remember that.

A motivating post for me comes from my Transformation Tuesday posts, where I show a picture of myself from 4 or 5 years ago, next to where I am today. Each time I post those, it really resonates, and I get new followers. For many of my followers, and the new followers I get daily, they just see me how I am now, and they don't see the "before" version of me. It shows how far I've come, and where I started, and motivates people to hang in there and start where they can start and go as far as they can go.

No matter what industry you're in, you always have a "before" spot. You can show an amateurish painting, or photograph, writing sample, or old video. Always showcase that "before," and where you are now. Maybe you were out of work five years ago, and now you're a self-made person. You can talk about that, show pictures or share a video. It helps bridge a gap between where your followers are right now, and where they would like to be. You influence someone by traveling down that road already, so you can inspire and motivate someone by sharing your story, and your travels, including your ups and downs, with them.

Sometimes what motivates someone is seeing what they don't want to be. When Josh was very young, maybe 9 years old, he was watching TV and eating chips while laying on the couch. His dad came in, with his big belly hanging over his waist, and said to Josh, "Keep that up, boy, and you'll look just like me," waving his belly around in jest. That's all it took for Josh, and he started his workout routine by doing push-ups and sit ups between commercials and lifting weights once he turned 12. Even though he started so young, and has always been in shape, he can still show transformation of muscle tone and development. For example, his senior year in high school to a more recent photo.

You can also inspire by telling client stories. For example, if you have a client who grants you permission to show or tell their transformation, that can be just as inspiring, maybe even more inspiring, than showing your own transformation. You can also show little steps of your transformation. For example, in fitness, before the Arnold Classic, I will really get it into gear for a "cutting" phase, so I can show my week by week progress as I work toward that mini-goal.

Telling your own personal story can always motivate someone if you've now achieved what they're looking for. My own personal story is a little different from Josh's. When I was in high school and college, I was very thin. I looked up to women on Instagram, like Amanda Latona, who were just strong. I thought to myself, "Man, I want to get there." I started buying these women's programs. Women I wanted to look like and women who inspired me. I started seeing results, sometimes just small improvements, and changes almost every single day, and found my motivation to keep at it, within. So, the women I was following really inspired my journey.

Whatever your story is, whether it comes from a personal tragedy, or something you overcame, or if it came from someone trying to beat you down, or someone helping you up. Tell that story and tell it honestly. Remind followers that when you share transformation photos or stories, whether of yourself or of others, that time will pass no matter what. One year will pass no matter what - do you want to be in better shape, or in a better place, a year from now? Then, here's what you can do, and I am going to help you.

What we notice is that committing to any single goal, fully and completely, affects other aspects of their life. In fitness, the dedication, a time commitment to achieving a physique that shows off absolute physical health, is intense. In relationships, that same level of commitment is necessary. If you can demonstrate the character and commitment to achieve important goals, it will naturally carry over into other aspects of your life. Followers really connect with that, and that type of motivation and inspiration can change lives. It's not just about getting shredded physically, more importantly, it's about character development that comes with it.

Before I really got serious with my Instagram account, there was a certain type of person that I was interested in following people who were successful at the sport that I was competing in. That built credibility for me. It then followed from there, like women who were successful in business, and who owned their own businesses, or who were successful in their relationships. I wasn't thinking about money right out of the gate. The money came organically as we developed ourselves and our businesses.

Don't necessarily only think about that when you're getting started. I sometimes feel that if you start your Instagram page with money in mind, you won't really develop a healthy following. Again, people kind of sniff that out, right away, and you won't build a raving fan base. People message me all the time asking about how they can build a following so that they can leave their job. I don't think you should build a following with that in mind. You should build a following to make the world a better place, and then the money will follow.

We chase value, not money. The more value you add to the marketplace, the more the marketplace will pay you. If you focus on the paying, and not the value, you won't add more value to the world. If you have a "taking" mentality, versus a "giving" mentality, people feel that, and they won't want to buy from you. They'll buy from someone else who has the giving mindset. That giving mindset comes from adding value to the world and making things better for people whether it's their products or services. Constantly asking yourself, how do I make this product better, or how do I make this service better? Focus on that value and philosophy, and you will build a successful Instagram following and a highly successful business.

Homework

Visit at least three of your favorite Instagram pages. What ratio do you notice with the variety of content?

_____

_____

_____

What are you most comfortable with posting?

_____

_____

_____

Least comfortable?

_____

_____

_____

How will you build your page to offer a variety of engaging content for your followers?

_____

_____

_____

How will you...

Motivate:

_____

Inspire:

_____

Inform:

_____

Use Humor:

_____

Entertain:

_____

Ask Followers to Take Action:

_____

Promote your Products and/or Services:

_____

"Go the extra mile, it's never crowded"

Chapter 13

Study Old Posts

A lot of people forget to do this, and don't reflect on how things worked, or didn't, as they build up their Instagram page. I know that if I didn't do this on a regular basis, looking over old posts and seeing how they did, I wouldn't have the following that I do.

I don't necessarily delete a post that didn't work or do very well. I might delete it to repost it on another day, or maybe as a "transformation" post. I do learn what people engage with, and I base my workout videos on that. For example, my back videos have the least engagement, so I don't really post a ton of those, because I don't think people really like those. The beauty of Instagram is that you'll know which posts work by looking at the level of engagement, the quality of comments, etc.

This is a great way to learn what people want and you can do that by studying old posts. For example, my transformation posts do really, really well. My recipe posts do really well. You have to really learn your following and understand your audience. Don't take this for granted or assume that your followers are stagnant and will only be interested in the same things over and over again. Just because recipe videos worked two years ago, doesn't mean they are as engaging now, for example. Looking at your old posts isn't something you do just once in a while, it's constant.

You'll also learn what translated better to a story, or to a live post, or to your blog, or your Instagram videos. Not only will you learn what content is most engaging, you will learn what format works. You'll also learn what times of the day, days of the week, work best. It's incredibly valuable information that is literally at your fingertips.

This brings up another reason and reinforcement that you don't outsource these types of activities. If you outsource this creative aspect, you will not learn all of this information, and your followers will either leave, or become disengaged, because you are just not paying enough attention. You're looking away, and not truly engaging and connecting with your audience.

Look at how many likes your posts get, how many shares or tags. Obviously pay attention to the number of comments, but also to the quality of comment. Is your post sparking conversation? For women in fitness, especially, is your post just sparking lewd comments? If so, you need to look at that and see what kind of followers you're attracting.

Resist the temptation to argue and engage with negativity, unless you are finding a way to turn it around. If it's really negative, I have no problem with deleting, or blocking. I am human, so it's natural to feel rage sometimes. Unfortunately, when you grow a large following, you have to expect this to some degree. Think of those people as broken and hurting, and they take it out on other people. Block and delete as you need, and don't let that negativity infiltrate who you are and what your page is about. Yes, you should stand up for yourself, but you shouldn't spend the majority of your day standing up for yourself.

You should spend the majority of your day interacting with the people who have your back. In fact, a mistake that both Josh and I have made is responding to negative posts, and effectively ignoring all the wonderfully amazing and supportive posts. By giving the negative attention, you attract more of the negative, because that's what's getting your attention. If you stop paying attention to the people who love you, guess what happens? They stop commenting, and they stop loving you? Kind of like life, isn't it?

We have a rule on our pages. If we comment back to a negative comment, we have to comment to every single positive comment that came before it. Since we've been doing that, we've been seeing and getting less and less negative posts. My block list is probably longer than some people's followers list. If you're not a part of my digital family, I don't have time for you. It's not just about collecting a number of followers, it's about nurturing a positive Instagram family. It's about protecting loving followers from hate and negativity. They don't want to visit a page like that, and neither would I. When I block certain individuals, it's not to protect me as much as it is to protect my digital friends. They don't need to put up with that.

Another way I deal with negativity is that whenever we are in the gym recording a workout, I try to make sure there is no one in the background. Inevitably, if there is, someone will comment about that person, and maybe make fun of their form, or what they're doing in the background. When that happens, I will always speak up for that person. One of the reasons people don't go to the gym is because they are afraid of being judged, so that type of behavior on my Instagram page is just not acceptable. I would never make fun of another person on my page, and I won't allow anyone else to, as well. Your page needs to be a safe place for your fans, and that is your responsibility. 100%. Protect your Instagram family.

How do you know a post is working? Is there a magic formula? Not really, because everyone's audience is different, and it does depend on how many followers you have. The number I look at is if I get a 1% reaction from my followers. To put that into numbers, if I have 1.2 million followers, I'm looking for about 12,000 points of engagement with that post.

If you have 10,000 followers, you should be getting 100 likes. If you're not getting that, then that post type is probably one you shouldn't repeat very often. We basically add our likes and comments together to figure this out - not necessarily "saves" or "shares" as much, because they're hard to track. Also, how quickly you're getting those likes. I might get 15,000 or 20,000 points of engagement on a post over the course of a week or month, but I'm mainly interested in what I get the first day of the post.

Instagram will most certainly change how things are tracked and as those features are developed, pay attention to them, so you can learn even more about who might be sharing your posts, or who is tagging you. As algorithms change, too, you have to adapt and make sure you're tuned into aspects and features that will help grow your raving fan base.

For YouTube channels, a great way to incentivize engagement is to say something like, "Hey, if you've added a comment, or engaged with my last five videos, you'll be entered into this next promotion or giveaway." Or, for a product, you can offer a giveaway or shout-out for people who purchase from you that week, or that month. Take the extra earnings to giveaway a cruise, or a trip for two somewhere.

You might clear an extra $15,000 and give away a $600 trip. How much fun is that?

The more engagement you can create, the more people will see your posts. The more people who see your posts, the more people you can help. You will need to giveaway a lot, especially for tax reasons, so talk to your accountant about this - make sure you have a good CPA when you start making money. We learned this the extremely hard way. The giveaways can really offset a lot of your profit, especially if you're offering soft services that don't have a lot of expenses attached to whatever income you receive.

Try a variety of giveaways and promotions and look back to see which ones were the most successful. Make sure your giveaways are something your fans will be interested in. If you are running an Instagram page about gardening, maybe you don't want to give away a hunting rifle. Give away a tool, or seeds, or a planting guide. It's a way to gamify your Instagram page, and increase engagement.

Learn from what created engagement, added fans, created more raving fans and built and improved your following. Even philanthropy posts can be highly successful and fit into our philosophy of making the world a better place. These types of posts can really build that raving fan-base that is critical to success on Instagram, or any other social media platform. Just be smart about what you think would build your brand the best, and the easiest way to figure that out is to study old posts, promotions and giveaways.

Homework

Study old posts on your page that did well- what common trends do you see?

_____

_____

_____

_____

_____

_____

_____

_____

_____

_____

_____

_____

_____

_____

_____

_____

_____

"The man who is prepared has his battle half fought"

Chapter 14

Five Questions You Should Ask Yourself Before You Post

You have 10,000 followers, or 100,000, or 1,000,000 followers now on Instagram. You got there by posting relevant information, entertaining content, helpful tips and engaging with your fans. You've created a raving fan base, and you're making money off of your platform by selling products and/or services. Can you see yourself there?

I've talked a lot about my "secrets" to building this kind of fan base, and creating an Instagram feed that will provide for you monetarily, and in your quest to make this world a better place. Engage, engage, engage. Do as many tasks yourself as you can and avoid outsourcing. Give away free information. Include humor and humanizing content. So, let's break that down a little bit more.

There are basically five things you should ask yourself before you post to your Instagram account.

What category is this post going to fall into? Inform, motivate, inspire, educate, promote? Make sure this is clear before you post. If it's not, sort out what would clarify your message, and if you need to, ask a trusted friend, first. Show them your post, and ask what they think the post is trying to be?

What's the goal of this post? To add value? To generate new fans? To boost engagement? Make sure your write your caption with that in mind, and that the accompanying picture or video helps you meet that goal?

Is this high quality? This doesn't mean polished and slick; you do want to show your human side. But, is the lighting decent? How about the sound? How does it look? Would you watch it if it weren't you?

Is your caption appropriate for the picture, and is the picture appropriate for the caption? Does it match the category of question 1? This is a really common mistake. If there's a mismatch, you will not have high engagement, and you may lose the attention of your followers.

Will this engage people?

The 5th question about engagement, I think, is the most important. Every post should engage people and help reach that 1% engagement goal that I set for all my posts. If it's a post that doesn't engage, I ask myself how I can make it more engaging. Sometimes a post is not designed to engage, so I will add a giveaway, as I talked about earlier. This engagement is critical on several counts because not only does a lack of engagement limit how many fans and raving fans you'll have, the Instagram algorithm will also place you lower in visibility and popularity, and fewer people will see and find you.

Go forth and engage. Build your Instagram following using these tips, and earn what you deserve by working hard, staying committed, taking care of your Instafamily, and being true to yourself. When you treat your Instagram pages like a job, you will find it will reward you. When you take care of your fans like they are treasured family, they will give you back to you. Listen and learn, constantly, and be authentic and human.

I hope this book helps you on your way, and I would love to hear from you and how you do. Please share what you learn with others and keep that giving mentality in all aspects of your life.

"It's a slow process, but quitting won't speed it up"

Thankyou for reading our book!

Made in the USA
Columbia, SC
23 December 2018